Legalines®

Editorial Advisors:
Gloria A. Aluise
Attorney at Law
Jonathan Neville
Attorney at Law
Robert A. Wyler
Attorney at Law

Authors:
Gloria A. Aluise
Attorney at Law
Daniel O. Bernstine
Attorney at Law
Roy L. Brooks
Professor of Law
Scott M. Burbank
C.P.A.
Charles N. Carnes
Professor of Law
Paul S. Dempsey
Professor of Law
Jerome A. Hoffman
Professor of Law
Mark R. Lee
Professor of Law
Jonathan Neville
Attorney at Law
Laurence C. Nolan
Professor of Law
Arpiar Saunders
Attorney at Law
Robert A. Wyler
Attorney at Law

D0701375

TORTS

Adaptable to Sixth Edition*
of Dobbs Casebook

By Jonathan Neville
Attorney at Law

*If your casebook is a newer edition, go to www.gilbertlaw.com
to see if a supplement is available for this title.

THOMSON REUTERS

EDITORIAL OFFICE: 1 N. Dearborn Street, Suite 650, Chicago, IL 60602
REGIONAL OFFICES: Chicago, Dallas, Los Angeles, New York, Washington, D.C.

SERIES EDITOR
Linda C. Schneider, J.D.
Attorney at Law

PRODUCTION MANAGER
Elizabeth G. Duke

FIRST PRINTING—2010

Legalines®

**Features Detailed Briefs of Every Major Case,
Plus Summaries of the Black Letter Law**

Titles Available

Administrative Law .... Keyed to Breyer
Administrative Law .... Keyed to Schwartz
Administrative Law .... Keyed to Strauss
Antitrust .... Keyed to Areeda
Antitrust .... Keyed to Pitofsky
Business Associations .... Keyed to Klein
Civil Procedure .... Keyed to Friedenthal
Civil Procedure .... Keyed to Hazard
Civil Procedure .... Keyed to Yeazell
Conflict of Laws .... Keyed to Currie
Constitutional Law .... Keyed to Brest
Constitutional Law .... Keyed to Choper
Constitutional Law .... Keyed to Rotunda
Constitutional Law .... Keyed to Stone
Constitutional Law .... Keyed to Sullivan
Constitutional Law .... Keyed to Varat
Contracts .... Keyed to Calamari
Contracts .... Keyed to Dawson
Contracts .... Keyed to Farnsworth
Contracts .... Keyed to Fuller
Contracts .... Keyed to Kessler
Contracts .... Keyed to Knapp
Contracts .... Keyed to Murphy
Corporations .... Keyed to Choper
Corporations .... Keyed to Eisenberg
Corporations .... Keyed to Hamilton

Criminal Law .... Keyed to Dressler
Criminal Law .... Keyed to Johnson
Criminal Law .... Keyed to Kadish
Criminal Law .... Keyed to Kaplan
Criminal Law .... Keyed to LaFave
Criminal Procedure .... Keyed to Kamisar
Domestic Relations .... Keyed to Wadlington
Estates and Trusts .... Keyed to Dobris
Evidence .... Keyed to Mueller
Evidence .... Keyed to Waltz
Family Law .... Keyed to Areen
Income Tax .... Keyed to Freeland
Income Tax .... Keyed to Klein
Labor Law .... Keyed to Cox
Property .... Keyed to Cribbet
Property .... Keyed to Dukeminier
Property .... Keyed to Nelson
Property .... Keyed to Rabin
Remedies .... Keyed to Rendelman
Securities Regulation .... Keyed to Coffee
Torts .... Keyed to Dobbs
Torts .... Keyed to Epstein
Torts .... Keyed to Franklin
Torts .... Keyed to Henderson
Torts .... Keyed to Prosser
Wills, Trusts & Estates .... Keyed to Dukeminier

All Titles Available at Your Law School Bookstore

 **THOMSON REUTERS**

SHORT SUMMARY OF CONTENTS

                                                                             Page

I.   **INTRODUCTION TO TORT LAW** 1

       A.   **Definitions and Distinctions** 1
       B.   **A Preliminary Look at the Process** 4

II.   **ESTABLISHING A CLAIM FOR INTENTIONAL TORT TO PERSON OR PROPERTY** 6

       A.   **Battery** 6
       B.   **Assault** 12
       C.   **False Imprisonment** 14
       D.   **Torts to Property** 16
       E.   **Civil Rights Violations** 21

III. **DEFENSES TO INTENTIONAL TORTS—PRIVILEGES** 23

       A.   **Self-Defense** 23
       B.   **Defense of Third Persons** 23
       C.   **Arrest and Detention** 24
       D.   **Defense and Repossession of Property** 25
       E.   **Discipline** 26
       F.   **Privileges** 26
       G.   **Privileges Not Based on Plaintiff's Conduct** 28

IV.   **NEGLIGENCE** 31

       A.   **Introduction** 31
       B.   **The Prima Facie Case for Negligence** 31
       C.   **Duty of Care** 31
       D.   **Specification of Particular Standards or Duties** 36
       E.   **Breach of Duty** 40
       F.   **Assessing Responsibility When More Than One Person Is Negligent** 44
       G.   **Proving and Evaluating Conduct** 45
       H.   **Res Ipsa Loquitur** 49
       I.   **Actual Harm** 53
       J.   **Cause in Fact** 54
       K.   **Proximate Cause** 60

V.   **DEFENSES TO NEGLIGENCE** 70

       A.   **Contributory Negligence** 70
       B.   **Comparative Negligence** 71
       C.   **Assumption of the Risk** 76

    D.   Statutes of Limitation   79

VI.   **LIMITING DUTY OF CARE ACCORDING TO CLASS OR STATUS OF THE PARTIES**   83

    A.   Introduction   83
    B.   Class or Status of Parties   83
    C.   Landowners   83
    D.   Lessors   91
    E.   Duties of Medical and Other Professionals   93
    F.   Immunities   103

VII.   **RELATIONSHIPS OR THEIR ABSENCE: NONACTION, CONTRACT, AND PROTECTION FROM OTHERS**   114

    A.   Nonfeasance and Misfeasance   114
    B.   Contract and Duty   119
    C.   The Duty to Protect From Third Persons   123

VIII.   **LIMITING DUTIES TO PROTECT AGAINST SPECIAL TYPES OF HARM**   130

    A.   Intentional Infliction of Emotional Distress   130
    B.   Negligent Infliction of Distress or Emotional Harm   132
    C.   Prenatal Harms   135
    D.   Wrongful Death and Survival   137

IX.   **VICARIOUS LIABILITY**   140

    A.   Introduction   140
    B.   Respondeat Superior and Scope of Employment   140
    C.   Employers Who Are Not Masters   144
    D.   Other Forms of Vicarious Responsibility   148

X.   **COMMON LAW STRICT LIABILITY**   150

    A.   Historical Development of Fault Liability   150
    B.   Nuisance   152
    C.   Unnatural Conditions on Land   155
    D.   Restatement Approaches   156
    E.   Defenses to Strict Liability   157

XI.   **PRODUCTS LIABILITY**   158

    A.   Theories of Recovery   158
    B.   Establishing a Prima Facie Case   163
    C.   Defenses and Related Issues   170

    D.   Extending Liability 175

XII. PRACTICAL LAWYERING PROBLEMS 177

    A.   Insurance and Settlement 177
    B.   Settlement and Trial Involving Multiple Defendants 180
    C.   Damages 186
    D.   Evaluating Tort Law 194

XIII. ALTERNATIVES TO TORT LAW 196

    A.   Workers' Compensation 196
    B.   Social Security Disability Benefits 202
    C.   Private Insurance 203
    D.   Evaluating Injury Systems 207

XIV. COMMUNICATION OF PERSONALLY HARMFUL
        IMPRESSIONS TO OTHERS 209

    A.   Defamation 209
    B.   Malicious Prosecution 216
    C.   Invasion of Privacy 218
    D.   Interference with Family Relations 220

XV. COMMUNICATION OF COMMERCIALLY HARMFUL
      IMPRESSIONS TO OTHERS 221

    A.   Injurious Falsehood 221
    B.   Intentional Interference with Contractual Relations 223
    C.   Trademark Infringement 227
    D.   Misappropriation of Commercial Value 228

XVI. MISREPRESENTATION AND OTHER MISDEALINGS 230

    A.   Theories of Liability 230
    B.   Basis of Liability 231
    C.   Opinion 232
    D.   Damages 233
    E.   Applications 233

TABLE OF CASES 237